Legends of Alola

By Simcha Whitehill

Legends of Alola

Written by Simcha Whitehill

The Prima Games logo and Primagames.com are registered trademarks of Penguin Random House LLC, registered in the United States. Prima Games is an imprint of DK, a division of Penguin Random House LLC, New York.

DK/Prima Games, a division of Penguin Random House LLC
6081 East 82nd Street, Suite #400
Indianapolis, IN 46250

ISBN: 978-0-7440-1945-2 (Paperback)
ISBN: 978-0-7440-1949-0 (Hardback)

Printing Code: The rightmost double-digit number is the year of the book's printing; the rightmost single-digit number is the number of the book's printing. For example, 18-1 shows that the first printing of the book occurred in 2018.
21 20 19 18   4 3 2 1

01-311217-Aug/2018
Printed and bound by Lake Book.

Credits

Publishing Manager
Tim Cox

Book Designer
Tim Amrhein

Production Designer
Tim Amrhein

Production
Beth Guzman

Prima Games Staff

VP
Mike Degler

Publisher
Mark Hughes

Licensing
Paul Giacomotto

Marketing Manager
Jeff Barton

Digital Publisher
Julie Asbury

Table of Contents

WHAT ARE LEGENDARY AND MYTHICAL POKÉMON?

Legendary and Mythical Pokémon are extremely rare and incredibly powerful. Each plays an important role in the history of the region and the peace of the whole world. Shrines and monuments are built to celebrate these unique and awesome Pokémon. Often, tales of their super strength are passed down through the generations. Only a very lucky few ever spot them from afar. But in this book, you will get a close-up look at some of the amazing Legendary and Mythical Pokémon of Alola.

ALL ABOUT THE ALOLA REGION

Alola! That word does not just mean "hello," it is also one of the most beautiful regions in the Pokémon world.

Alola is made up of a group of islands. Each one is filled with amazing beaches, greenery and, of course, incredible Pokémon. There are four main islands: Melemele, Ula'ula, Poni, and Akala.

Pokémon fans should not miss the chance to visit Alola. Many Pokémon here have unique Alolan Forms special to the region. Their names and species stay the same, but their appearance and abilities are different.

Curious students who want to learn all about Pokémon and Alola can join the famous Pokémon School on Melemele Island. There, Pokémon researcher Professor Samson Oak and Professor Kukui teach classes.

However, it is hard to stay indoors in a region that offers so much to explore outdoors. So, students of the Pokémon School often go on fun field trips. Alola is also the perfect place for people and Pokémon who love to swim, hike, row, trek, water ski, jet ski, and enjoy the great outdoors.

There are so many natural wonders to explore from the blue seas to the green mountains. It is no surprise many tourists come here on vacation. Alola is the region for fun in the sun!

THE ISLAND GUARDIANS

In Alola, a special group of Pokémon known as the Island Guardians protects the balance of nature on each island.

These four Legendary Pokémon play an important role in maintaining both the land and spirit of Alola. Tapu Koko looks over Melemele Island. Tapu Lele cares for Akala Island. Tapu Fini watches Poni Island. Tapu Bulu looks after Ula'ula Island.

TAPU KOKO

Tapu Koko is the Island Guardian, or Spirit Guardian, of Melemele Island. The Electric- and Fairy-type soars through the sky with wings that act as a protective shield.In a snap, it can tuck its body between the two halves of its shell shield, making it hard for a foe to land a blow.

It is rare that one would be lucky enough to see Tapu Koko. It is even more difficult to follow the Legendary Pokémon, especially in a battle. Tapu Koko moves so quickly, it is impossible to follow with your eyes.

Tapu Koko is also known for something besides its amazing speed. The Island Guardian can call upon storm clouds and gather their lightening for strength. It can then carry the charges from the bolts inside its body and use them to blast back an opponent.

Beware of angering Tapu Koko. It has a fiery temper that is easy to trigger. As the Island Guardian, it is always on alert and ready to roll. Although the Legendary Pokémon is not known to hold a grudge, Tapu Koko has a short temper and an even shorter memory.

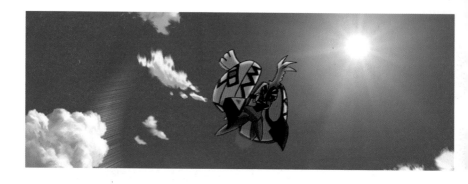

As the protector of Melemele Island, Tapu Koko's curious nature comes in handy. It is full of wonder, ready to explore or sniff out any situation. Brave Tapu Koko keeps a lookout over its homeland and stays informed. Melemele Island is lucky to have the watchful eye and big heart of its Legendary Spirit Guardian, Tapu Koko.

TAPU LELE

If you spot a spray of rainbow-colored sparkles in the sky, you could follow the trail to see Tapu Lele. The Spirit Guardian of Akala Island releases shining scales as it travels.

While they are beautiful to behold, they can give a speedy recovery for an injured person or Pokémon. The Land Spirit Pokémon's twinkling scales have the power to heal.

So, if you find yourself feeling weak on Akala Island, look for Tapu Lele. This Pokémon's scales can instantly act like a visit to Nurse Joy at the Pokémon Center.

The power of the Psychic- and Fairy-type Pokémon's scales are so great, it is said that they once repaired all of Alola! According to local legend, the islands were locked in a horrible war. The warriors were tired and hurting, but they would not give up their fight.

That is until Tapu Lele spread its shining scales and healed the soldiers' bodies and their spirits. The Legendary Pokémon brought the war to an end.

Where does Tapu Lele get its soothing strength? The Legendary Pokémon powers up with the perfume of the pretty flowers around Alola. Their sweet scent is its source of energy.

Even though it ended that epic war, Tapu Lele is no stranger to battle. It has a reputation for fighting too rough because it does not know its own strength. At 3'11" tall and 41 pounds, it packs a surprising punch. Tapu Lele does not like to battle unless it knows it can win.

TAPU BULU

You can hear the island guardian of Ula'ula coming from a mile away! That's because Tapu Bulu rings its tail to show it is nearby. It likes to announce its arrival by sound since it is afraid its fierce 6'03" appearance might scare people and Pokémon. So, it would rather lead with a chime than frighten all the time.

Tapu Bulu is not known to pick a fight. In fact, it is known for being relaxed. Some have called this Legendary lazy. When the 100.3-pound Pokémon enters battle, it holds nothing back. Tapu Bulu does not give mercy to its foes.

According to Alolan legend, Tapu Bulu once attacked a band of thieves who were robbing its shrine by swinging tall trees like they were bats.

Tapu Bulu is a Grass- and Fairy-type that has a unique power over plants. It can make any sprout grow and gain strength from the greenery. The island guardian can also use this gift on itself to make its wooden horns bigger, tougher, and even a different shape.

Tapu Bulu's typical battle strategy is to use plants to tie down its opponents. Once the foe is trapped, Tapu Bulu will use its horns to deliver a powerful blow.

TAPU FINI

The island guardian of Poni Island is Tapu Fini. It draws its power from the pull of the mighty sea's currents. The Legendary

Tapu Fini can control the flow of water. It even uses water against its enemies in battle. It avoids the deep end of a clash. Instead, Tapu Fini will send a heavy fog to make its foes fight themselves.

If the Legendary Pokémon does accept a battle challenge, it might seem bored. After all, it does have a special skill that causes many to come together to challenge Tapu Fini.

The Land Spirit Pokémon of Poni Island can create pure water that can cleanse anything, even body and soul. It is no wonder so many seek Tapu Fini's famous filtered water. Sadly, not all visitors have the best intentions.

Many villains have tried to steal this water, but Tapu Fini is prepared. It has developed a trial to make out their true goal. The Legendary Pokémon drops a dense fog that can crush anyone with evil plans. If someone does need the help of Tapu Fini's terrific water, it will pass the test and take the heat of its super steam.

Tapu Fini is not easy to find. It tries to avoid people, perhaps as a way to protect its purified water. After all, Tapu Fini has defeated its fair share of foes. The Legendary Pokémon is too wise and tough to let anyone take advantage of its liquid gift.

NECROZMA AND ITS FIERCE FORMS

Standing at 7'10" tall, Necrozma is a giant and powerful Pokémon said to be from a different world. The Psychic-type prefers to

sleep underground. When it is on the surface, it is hard to miss. The Legendary Pokémon can put on quite a laser light show. Necrozma shoots blasts of rainbow light from its two massive arms.

The Prism Pokémon uses light energy it saps from its foes to launch colorful lasers. While they may look pretty, it can get ugly. Necrozma's laser beams can blast through anything!

This 507.1-pound Legendary Pokémon is not shy. It is always ready to show it is prepared to fight.

Necrozma is known to go on rampages in search of the light energy it needs. Those who have seen it in such a state have said that it seems to suffer when it is weak. Depending on the light energy Necrozma finds, it could take on three more forms: Dusk Mane Necrozma, Dawn Wings Necrozma, or Ultra Necrozma.

DUSK MANE NECROZMA

When it feasts on The Sunne Pokémon Solgaleo's intense light energy, it takes on the form of Dusk Mane Necrozma.

It doubles in weight reaching 1014.1 pounds and grows to 12'06" tall.

The Psychic- and Steel-type's four feet have ferocious claws. If a foe tries to sneak up from behind, it will be in for a terrible surprise.

DAWN WINGS NECROZMA

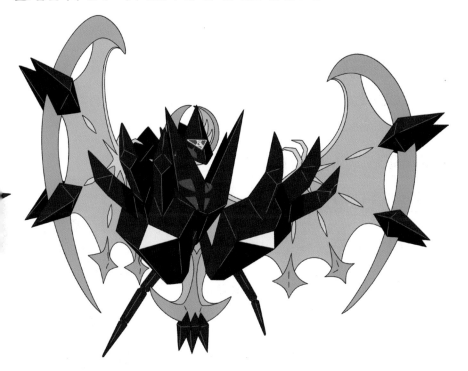

In complete control of Lunala, it takes the form of Dawn Wings Necrozma. Stealing Legendary Pokémon Lunala's light energy makes this Form a fierce force.

The Psychic- and Ghost-type is a gigantic 13'09" tall and weighs 771.6 pounds.

ULTRA NECROZMA

Like a tower on two legs, Ultra Necrozma is 24'07" tall! The Psychic- and Dragon-type remains 507.1 pounds because of what caused the growth spurt.

It takes this incredible Form when it is overfilled with an extreme amount of light energy. Due to its incredible power, laser beams fire from every edge of its body. These bright light beams impact the natural world in a very unusual way.

THE SYNTHETIC POKÉMON
TYPE: NULL

Wild Type: Null wears a solid helmet to help control its anger. It seems the only thing as great as its rage is its super strength. All 6'03" and 265.7 pounds of Type: Null was manufactured. It is known as the Synthetic Pokémon.

The reason
Type: Null was
created is a
mystery. However,
it seems to be
filled with
deep anger.

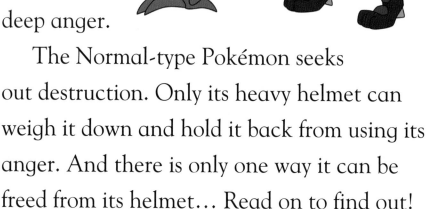

The Normal-type Pokémon seeks
out destruction. Only its heavy helmet can
weigh it down and hold it back from using its
anger. And there is only one way it can be
freed from its helmet… Read on to find out!

SILVALLY

Only when Type: Null finds true
friendship with its Trainer can its heart
and helmet be unlocked. Then, and only
then, can it evolve and become Silvally.
The connection between Silvally and its
Trainer is deep.

The Legendary Pokémon will even risk its life to protect its beloved best friend. According to myth, the boy who first helped it evolve into this Form gave it the name Silvally.

Once free from the weight of its helmet, Silvally will see an increase in its speed and senses. The Synthetic Pokémon will also lose its anger and its true nature will return. Silvally will trust its Trainer to be its guide. In this form, Silvally can truly meet its destiny and defend the world.

Silvally has an amazing Ability to help it in its mission! In its natural state, Silvally stands 7'07" tall, weighs 221.6 pounds, and is a Normal-type.

However, it has the power to change its type. When special chips are inserted into a drive on its head, its RKS System will glow with a color showing its new type. Silvally can then make a temporary type shift. Silvally is the first Pokémon to have this incredible RKS System Ability. The state of the world depends on its strength!

THE EXCITING EVOLUTION OF COSMOG

Tiny Cosmog is eight inches tall. The only thing smaller than the size of this Pokémon is the number of Alolans who know it exists. According to myth, only Kings and royalty had heard about Cosmog. It is believed to be from another world.

Today, researchers at the Aether Foundation in Alola have begun to study this amazing Legendary Pokémon. A scientist gave it the name Cosmog. A Psychic-type, it is also known as the Nebula Pokémon.

Cosmog's body is made of gas and weighs a mere 0.2 pounds. It is so lightweight that it goes with the flow of the wind.

As it travels through the air, Cosmog collects dust and light that can make its body bigger.

COSMOEM

Cosmoem may only be four inches tall, but don't try to pick it up! The  Protostar Pokémon weighs a ton; a ton plus some. Cosmoem weighs 2204.4 pounds!

What makes Cosmoem so heavy is unknown. Its body has a pitch-black center surrounded by a mysterious substance covered in a solid casing. The Psychic Pokémon is said to be from another world. Long ago, Cosmoem was called the "cocoon of the stars."

Cosmoem is not known for bouncing around. In fact, it does not move. One way to tell it is a living Legendary Pokémon is by the gentle heat given off by its body.

SOLGALEO

The Legendary Pokémon Solgaleo is an evolved form of Cosmoem. Thought to be from another world, it returns to its homeland when the third eye on its forehead glows.

Solgaleo is 11'02" tall and it weighs 507.1 pounds. Those who have seen this magical Psychic- and Steel-type Pokémon believe its massive mane resembles the sun. In fact, it is called The Sunne Pokémon.

Solgaleo can store so much power in its body that it can shine a bright light that can turn dark night into noon. Because of this incredible gift, it is thought to be the messenger of the sun.

LUNALA

Legendary Pokémon Lunala's bright arms look like crescent moons. Those lucky enough to have seen this extraordinary Pokémon say that when The Moon Pokémon stretches out its arms, it looks just like the night sky.

Lunala is so powerful it can turn bright day into pure darkness. Because of this, it is said to be the messenger of the moon.

Lunala is an evolved form of Cosmoem. It is a Psychic- and Ghost-type, weighs 264.6 pounds, and is 13'01" tall.

At the top of its head is a third eye. When it flashes, Lunala flies off to another world—a world thought to be its true home.

MARSHADOW

Standing at 2'04" tall and weighing 48.9 pounds, the Mythical Pokémon Marshadow has a big advantage! It is the first known Pokémon that is both a dual Fighting- and Ghost-type.

Marshadow is called the Gloomdweller Pokémon. From the cover of a shadowy spot, it likes to study a Pokémon's every move, thought, and strength. It learns all about the Pokémon so it can copy it. Then, like an award-winning actor, it delivers a perfect performance.

QUIZ

1. Which Legendary Pokémon is commonly referred to as The Moone Pokémon?

2. Which Legendary Pokémon is thought to be the male evolved form of Cosmoem?

3. The Island Guardian Tapu Koko looks after which island?

4. Which Pokémon feasts on The Sunne Pokémon Solgaleo's intense light energy?

5. Which Pokémon can make a temporary type shift?

6. Where have researchers begun to study the Legendary Pokémon Cosmog?

Glossary

Absorb
To soak up or drink in.

Dual
Composed or consisting of two items or parts.

Evolve
Develop or change. In the Pokémon world, it's when a Pokémon changes into its next form.

Guardian
A person (or thing) who guards, protects, or preserves.

Mythical
Pertaining to or involving a myth. In the Pokémon world, Mythical Pokémon are event-exclusive Pokémon that, with few exceptions, cannot be obtained during normal gameplay.

Psychic
Special mental powers to read minds or predict the future.

Recovery
Return to health from sickness.

Region
An area or section of a country or world.

Temper
A state of mind, sometimes shown in outbursts of anger.

Answers to the Quiz: 1. Lunala; 2. Solgaleo; 3. Melemele Island; 4. Dusk Mane Necrozma; 5. Silvally; 6. Aether Foundation.

31

A LEVEL FOR EVERY READER

This book is a part of an exciting four-level reading series to support children in developing the habit of reading widely for both pleasure and information. Each book is designed to develop a child's reading skills, fluency, grammar awareness, and comprehension in order to build confidence and enjoyment when reading.

Ready for a Level 2 (Beginning to Read) book
A child should:
- be able to recognize a bank of common words quickly and be able to blend sounds together to make some words.
- be familiar with using beginner letter sounds and context clues to figure out unfamiliar words.
- sometimes correct his/her reading if it doesn't look right or make sense.
- be aware of the need for a slight pause at commas and a longer one at periods.

A valuable and shared reading experience
For many children, reading requires much effort, but adult participation can make reading both fun and easier. Here are a few tips on how to use this book with a young reader:

Check out the contents together:
- read about the book on the back cover and talk about the contents page to help heighten interest and expectation.
- discuss new or difficult words.
- chat about labels, annotations, and pictures.

Support the reader:
- give the book to the young reader to turn the pages.
- where necessary, encourage longer words to be broken into syllables, sound out each one, and then flow the syllables together; ask him/her to reread the sentence to check the meaning.
- encourage the reader to vary her/his voice as she/he reads; demonstrate how to do this if helpful.

Talk at the end of each book, or after every few pages:
- ask questions about the text and the meaning of the words used—this helps develop comprehension skills.
- read the quiz at the end of the book and encourage the reader to answer the questions, if necessary, by turning back to the relevant pages to find the answers.

Series consultant, Dr. Linda Gambrell, Emerita Distinguished Professor of Education at Clemson University, has served as President of the National Reading Conference, the College Reading Association, and the International Reading Association.